Milet Publishing
Smallfields Cottage, Cox Green
Rudgwick, Horsham, West Sussex
RH12 3DE England
info@milet.com
www.milet.com
www.milet.co.uk

First English–Spanish edition published by Milet Publishing in 2013

ISBN 978 1 84059 832 2

Original Turkish text written by Erdem Seçmen
Translated to English by Alvin Parmar and adapted by Milet

Illustrated by Chris Dittopoulos
Designed by Christangelos Seferiadis

Printed and bound in Turkey by Ertem Matbaası

My Bilingual Book

Taste
El gusto

English–Spanish

Close your eyes, taste this drink . . .

Cierra los ojos. Toma un sorbito . . .

Water or soda, what do you think?

¿Agua o limonada? Piensa un poquito.

How do you know which one it is?

¿Cuál de ellas, de repente,

Do your mouth and tongue feel a fizz?

te hace cosquillas entre los dientes?

Your mouth and tongue let you taste drinks and food.

Con la boca y la lengua percibes todos los sabores:

They tell you what tastes bad and what tastes good!

los buenos, los malos e incluso los peores.

Your taste senses bitter, sour, sweet,

Sabor ácido, dulce, amargo o salado.

and salty, like the crackers you eat.

Cada alimento tiene un sabor distinto y variado.

Some like the taste of chocolate best.

El chocolate sabe delicioso,

Most like the taste of medicine less!

pero la medicina sabe horroroso.

It's fun to think about yummy sweets,

Los dulces tienen un sabor excelente.

but eating too many is bad for your teeth!

Si tomas demasiados es malo para tus dientes.

Foods like peppers can be so hot!

Un chile muy picante puede darte un susto.

Your taste will tell you to eat them or not.

Por eso debes confiar en el sentido del gusto.

Some tastes go together and some really don't mix,

Algunos sabores combinan bien, otros combinan mal.

like that banana and cheese sandwich you are about to fix!

Banana con queso... Quizás una pizca de sal.

These delicious fruits deserve a nibble.

Frutas de sabores y colores increíbles.

They're good for your body and irresistible!

Son muy sanas y totalmente irresistibles.

Trying different foods makes your taste sense grow.

Educa tu gusto y prueba muchísimos alimentos:

Your world gets bigger, the more foods that you know!

tu mente se ampliará y tu cuerpo estará contento.